Designed and produced by
Aladdin Books Ltd
70 Old Compton Street
London W1

Design: Rob Hillier
Editor: Margaret Fagan
Researcher: Cecilia Weston-Baker

First published in the
United States in 1989 by
Gloucester Press
387 Park Avenue South
New York, NY 10016

ISBN 0 531 17138 8

Printed in Belgium

The front cover shows the London
Stock Market on Black Monday,
October 19, 1987. The back cover
shows the dealing room in Japan.

Library of Congress Catalog
Card Number: 88-83096

The author, Mihir Bose, *has written several books on a variety of*
subjects including The Crash – the first study of Black Monday and
its consequences. He was deputy editor of Financial Weekly *and*
features editor of London Daily News, *both in Britain. He now*
writes for the British national newspapers on business matters.

The consultant, Alan Weber Ph.D, *is currently research fellow for*
the Securities Industry Program at the Business School of the City
University in London, England. He was coauthor of A Monetary
History of the U.K. 1870-1982 *and related articles.*

The publishers wish to thank Nick Thompson for his help in producing this book.

Contents

Introduction	4
The money crisis?	6
The role of technology	8
The domestic market	10
The currency factor	12
Interest rates	14
Inflation	16
Buy now, pay later	18
Money worldwide	20
Market economics	22
The communist system	24
Developing countries	26
Could it happen again?	28
Money facts	30
Index	32

CRASH !

A NEW MONEY CRISIS ?

MIHIR BOSE

Illustrated by
Ron Hayward Associates

GLOUCESTER PRESS
New York : London : Toronto : Sydney

Introduction

On Monday October 19, 1987, the value of share prices on the New York Stock Exchange in Wall Street fell by a record amount: a staggering 22.6 percent of the value of the exchange was wiped out in one day's trading. The day was dubbed Black Monday and triggered a chain of events that shook all the world's major stock markets.

In the past, stock prices had gone up for a time, then fallen. Yet, in the five years leading to Black Monday, the world's stock markets saw an almost uninterrupted rise in the value of stocks. Everyone was optimistic that, perhaps, stock prices could always be made to go up. Before Black Monday everyone was trying to buy stocks. Then suddenly everyone wanted to sell and all the world's stock markets fell sharply.

Opinions varied about the impact of the crash. Would it be the start of an international money crisis and economic decline? After all, the 1929 Wall Street crash heralded a worldwide depression, with large numbers of unemployed, widespread poverty and misery. This book is about what happened in the 1987 crash. It explains the world's money system and why people fear the crash's impact on their own money.

▷ The dealing room of the New York exchange on the day of the crash – the graph shows how sharply prices fell.

What is a stock?

Investors can buy stocks in a company. In return they expect a proportion of any profit the company makes. When a company makes a profit, demand to own its stocks increases and many stocks are bought and sold. If confidence fails, investors may also rush to sell their stocks.

4

Black Monday
The graph shows both the
scale of the fall and the speed
with which stock prices fell.

10.00 11.00 12.00 13.00 14.00 15.00 16.00

The money crisis ?

The 1987 crash was triggered by fears that the economic problems faced by the United States were going to get worse. The U.S. spends more than it receives ("budget deficit") and this is a cause for alarm. As investors worried, they sold their stocks. Stock prices in other countries then crashed, partly because of fears that the economic problems in the United States would reduce trade in the rest of the world.

The United States has by far the world's largest economy. Investors reasoned that if Americans had less money and therefore spent less, then other countries would not be able to sell as many goods to the U.S.

But there were other worries about the U.S. economic situation – namely the "trade deficit." The United States was importing too much from other countries and not exporting enough. Stronger demands for import controls in the United States raised fears that if imports were restricted then other countries would do the same. This would disrupt the delicate balance of world trade. Countries with a strong export-led economy would then need to find new markets for their goods or factories would close and unemployment would follow. This could lead to another world recession.

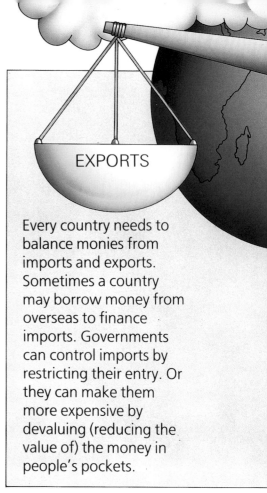

EXPORTS

Every country needs to balance monies from imports and exports. Sometimes a country may borrow money from overseas to finance imports. Governments can control imports by restricting their entry. Or they can make them more expensive by devaluing (reducing the value of) the money in people's pockets.

Countries earn money when they export more than they import (trade surplus), and through banking, insurance services and tourism (invisible earnings). Together with surplus money raised through taxes, these make up a country's "reserves."

Depression years

◁ After the 1929 Wall Street crash, the United States introduced import controls to protect its economy. Other governments panicked and also restricted imports. This interfered with world trade. The effect was to stop the

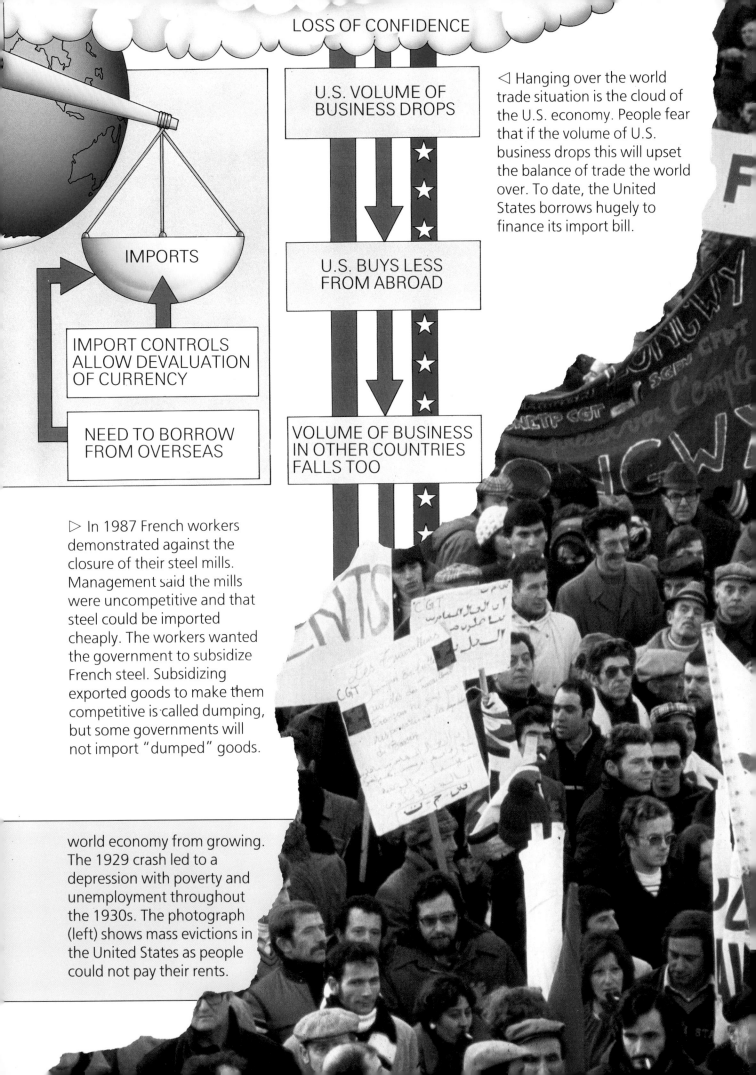

LOSS OF CONFIDENCE

IMPORTS

IMPORT CONTROLS ALLOW DEVALUATION OF CURRENCY

NEED TO BORROW FROM OVERSEAS

U.S. VOLUME OF BUSINESS DROPS

U.S. BUYS LESS FROM ABROAD

VOLUME OF BUSINESS IN OTHER COUNTRIES FALLS TOO

◁ Hanging over the world trade situation is the cloud of the U.S. economy. People fear that if the volume of U.S. business drops this will upset the balance of trade the world over. To date, the United States borrows hugely to finance its import bill.

▷ In 1987 French workers demonstrated against the closure of their steel mills. Management said the mills were uncompetitive and that steel could be imported cheaply. The workers wanted the government to subsidize French steel. Subsidizing exported goods to make them competitive is called dumping, but some governments will not import "dumped" goods.

world economy from growing. The 1929 crash led to a depression with poverty and unemployment throughout the 1930s. The photograph (left) shows mass evictions in the United States as people could not pay their rents.

The role of technology

Worries about the state of the U.S. economy would explain some, but not all, of the reasons for the fall on Black Monday. A popular theory was that the speed with which the New York market fell was due to the effects of computers. The 1929 crash hit just New York and it was many months before it spread round the world.

The old dealing rooms where traders met face to face have disappeared. In their place hundreds of dealing rooms have opened where all deals are made using the telephone or a computer. Just as credit cards make it easier for us to spend money, impersonal dealing facilities promote vast international trading in shares.

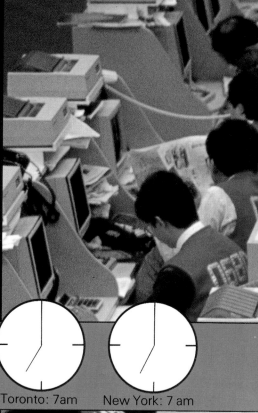

▷ The 24 hour clock shows that when Tokyo is about to close for the day London is at lunch and waiting to see how New York will open.

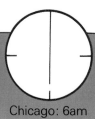

Chicago: 6am   Toronto: 7am   New York: 7 am

The new technology means that investors can buy and sell stocks at the push of a button and this encourages the gambling instinct. It worked all right as long as stock prices were rising but when they started to fall the computers were programmed to sell and millions of stocks were sold in the panic. "Program trading" made gambling easier.

Before Black Monday many experts had predicted that Japan's stock market might fall. Stock prices were far too high and many people had borrowed money to buy stocks. But the Japanese market has no program trading. Instead the government keeps a tight control and its stocks did not fall as sharply as elsewhere in the world.

▽ The photograph shows the dealing room on the Japanese stock market.

London: noon   Paris: 1pm   Germany: 1pm   Hong Kong: 8pm   Tokyo: 9pm   Sydney: 10pm

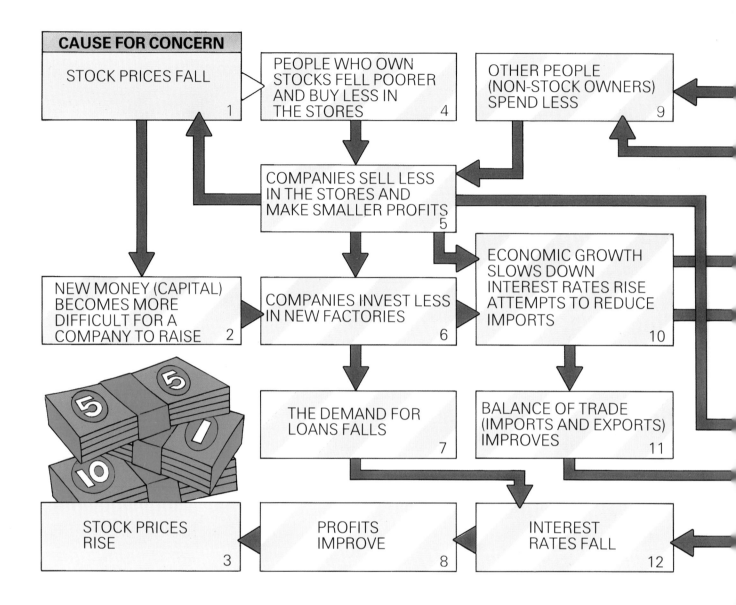

CAUSE FOR CONCERN

STOCK PRICES FALL **1**	PEOPLE WHO OWN STOCKS FELL POORER AND BUY LESS IN THE STORES **4**	OTHER PEOPLE (NON-STOCK OWNERS) SPEND LESS **9**

COMPANIES SELL LESS IN THE STORES AND MAKE SMALLER PROFITS **5**

NEW MONEY (CAPITAL) BECOMES MORE DIFFICULT FOR A COMPANY TO RAISE **2**	COMPANIES INVEST LESS IN NEW FACTORIES **6**	ECONOMIC GROWTH SLOWS DOWN INTEREST RATES RISE ATTEMPTS TO REDUCE IMPORTS **10**
	THE DEMAND FOR LOANS FALLS **7**	BALANCE OF TRADE (IMPORTS AND EXPORTS) IMPROVES **11**
STOCK PRICES RISE **3**	PROFITS IMPROVE **8**	INTEREST RATES FALL **12**

How a crash can effect the economy

The diagram shows the different outcomes of a drop in stock prices (1). When stock prices collapse this affects wealth and jobs. Two effects are most feared: the wealth effect (4, 5, 9) and the investment effect (5, 6, 7 and 10). A fall in stock prices can mean that the company cannot sell its stocks. As a result companies find it difficult to raise money to expand in the way they had planned (10). The diagram also shows how factors outside the stock market can upset the money system. These include raising taxes on both industry and individuals as well as large-scale spending by the state on public services.

The domestic market

CAUSE FOR CONCERN

HIGH TAXES AND
PUBLIC SPENDING
13

UNEMPLOYMENT
RISES
14

PROSPECTS FOR
COMPANIES LOOK
GLOOMY
15

INFLATION
FALLS
16

CURRENCY
STRENGTHENS
17

Black Monday made everyone realize how fragile the international and domestic money system is. Many people lost money as they sold their stocks – every American family was said to be $14,000 poorer.

Business feared that if people were poorer, or thought they were poorer, they would spend less. This would reduce the sales of goods and services (wealth effect). Many business people began to reassess plans for expansion (investment effect). Experts in the stock markets became very gloomy about how much money a company would make in the future and marked down their stocks. Some companies were so badly affected that their stock price halved.

These were the immediate fears of the 1987 crash on the stock market. But what people really feared was the onset of a severe long-term economic depression, like the one that devastated Europe and the United States in the 1930s, after the panic selling on Wall Street.

However, the effects of the 1987 crash have been limited. It seems the fear that gripped the stock market on Black Monday had not started the reaction that could lead to a domestic recession (see number 10 in the diagram). International cooperation was vital to stop the panic and strengthen the markets, some of which have now recovered. Yet the crash has left the markets "jittery" and seeking reassurance.

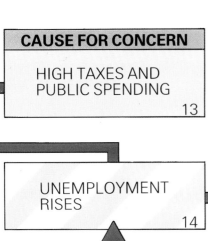

◁ The state of a country's economy affects how much money people have. Prices of everyday items such as food are determined by the factors illustrated in the diagram.

The currency factor

Any upset in world trade affects the international money system. This is because the money system is a "mirror image" of the trading system – goods are almost always exchanged for money, not directly for other goods.

But different countries use different kinds of money, or currency. It is possible to swap, for example, U.S. dollars for Japanese yen or British pounds for German marks, by buying and selling money on the "money market" organized by the banks. The exchange rate (how many dollars you get for one yen) is affected by: trade (the buying and selling of goods from overseas); the cost of money (interest); and speculative demand (how many people want to enter the market of buying and selling money).

Because of the crash, and predictions that the level of international trade would drop, each country feared that its own currency would drop in value relative to others. If all the world's governments had reacted separately, they probably would have raised interest rates (see page 14) to reduce the supply of their own nation's money in an attempt to stop the value of their currency falling.

The Dollar's decline
▽ The graph shows the percentage the dollar, pound and yen rise and fall in relation to each other in all the currency markets of the world. In recent times it is the dollar that has fallen in value against the yen (by 48 percent) and the pound (by 38 percent).

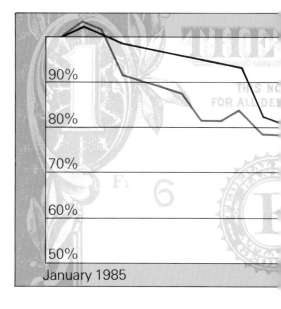

90%

80%

70%

60%

50%

January 1985

◁ The photogaph shows crowds waiting on Wall Street in 1929. After the 1929 crash, governments clamped down on the supply of money to try and maintain the value of their currency. But everyone did it and the values of different currencies relative to each other did not change very much. The shortage of money meant that business slowed down so badly that the world economy almost stopped.

But raising interest rates caused disaster in 1929. So in 1987 countries cooperated to ensure there was enough money available in the world to keep business going. (Raising interest rates means that saving money in a bank becomes more attractive, so more money is deposited and kept out of circulation and off the stock market.) The only worry was that keeping plenty of money going around in the system, while the level of business was expected to fall, would lead to inflation.

"What happens if a currency falls in value?"

– Foreign goods and raw materials become more expensive. Prices may rise, and people are less well off. People may buy more home products.

– Foreign travel becomes more expensive.

– Speculators expecting further falls in the value sell more of the currency, so that its value falls further.

– Unless governments act to buy their own currency using reserves (national earnings) or foreign currency earned by exports, the value of the currency can slide down unchecked and the amount of currency in the country can be reduced. Raising or lowering interest rates (see overleaf) also controls the value of currency in the system.

48% drop

38% drop

Fall against the pound

Fall against the yen

January 1987

January 1988

△ Changes in currency can make vacations overseas more expensive.

Interest rates

An interest rate is the price paid by someone who borrows money and received by someone who lends it. Business people borrow money from the bank, and many consumers use credit cards to buy cars, clothes, foreign vacations, and a host of other goods and services. Interest must be paid on all these borrowings. The amount of interest paid depends on how much money is borrowed, how long it is borrowed for, and who it is borrowed from.

The government has some control over the economy by changing interest rates. If it feels that it would like people to spend more, then it lowers interest rates. As interest rates go down people feel they can afford to borrow more, so they can spend more on credit and don't save. If the government feels people are spending too much so that the country is buying in too many foreign goods, then it may increase interest rates.

Money supply

Governments can do many things to affect the price and availability of money:
— change interest rates
— directly control credit
— indirectly control credit (lending restrictions)
— print more or less money
— raise taxes
— cut public spending
— set up exchange rate controls

But many governments rely almost entirely on changing interest rates.

This has two effects. In the short term, people save more and have less money to spend. They therefore spend less on foreign goods. In the long term, the value of the home currency eventually increases and so imports become cheaper and people buy more.

On Naeoya Wharf, Japan, cars are waiting to be exported to the United States. Some U.S. politicians call for restricted imports.

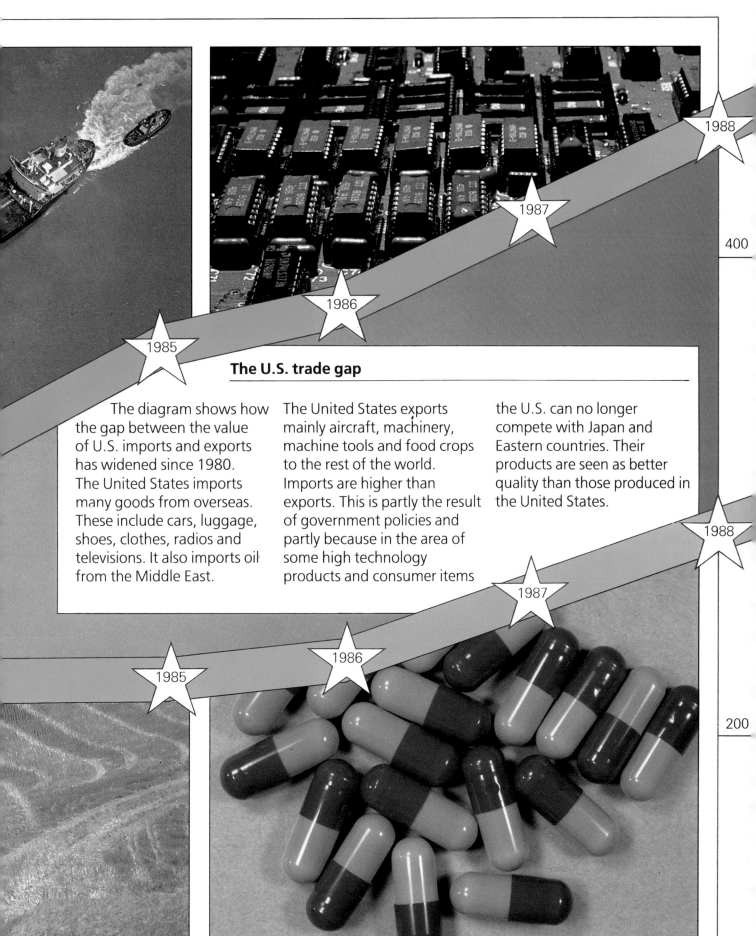

The U.S. trade gap

The diagram shows how the gap between the value of U.S. imports and exports has widened since 1980. The United States imports many goods from overseas. These include cars, luggage, shoes, clothes, radios and televisions. It also imports oil from the Middle East.

The United States exports mainly aircraft, machinery, machine tools and food crops to the rest of the world. Imports are higher than exports. This is partly the result of government policies and partly because in the area of some high technology products and consumer items the U.S. can no longer compete with Japan and Eastern countries. Their products are seen as better quality than those produced in the United States.

Money worldwide

The 1987 crash made people realize that international disruption of trade and finance is dangerous and that governments have to intervene. They are the only ones who can! Before the crash, many governments relaxed or abolished foreign exchange controls so vast sums of money could flow easily from one country to another. At present, there are few checks and balances to help the system avoid high risks. Today many governments are alarmed and demand greater controls on the movement of money on the stock markets.

But are all countries in the world vulnerable to what happens on the stock markets? Those countries who run their economies based on the ideas of free trade or market economics (see opposite) are those most affected. They take risks on the stock market – and make gains. The communist countries such as the Soviet Union believe that stock markets involve unnecessary competition and have a planned economy. However even they are moving toward allowing market forces to influence their economies.

Capitalist countries
Most companies are privately owned and have to compete in the marketplace to sell their products and services. Free trade allows unrestricted imports and exports.

Communist countries
Under this system the state owns all industry and services. This means that industry is planned by the state and there is no competition between rival companies.

Developing countries
These produce basic commodities like sugar. The crops are grown and harvested using a great deal of labor and often do not fetch high prices on the international market.

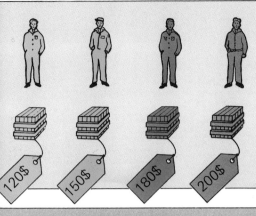

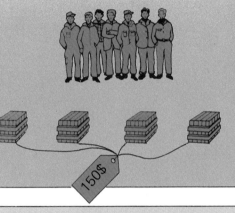

Under this system many different companies produce goods, such as cars. Each car has a different price and consumers can choose the type of car and the amount they will pay.

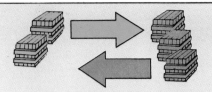

The aim is to export. But if factories cannot meet domestic demand, goods will be imported.

Because the state owns industry, the price range and types of different products for sale is smaller. Planning can also lead to gluts and shortages if demand changes quickly.

Exports and imports are only encouraged to earn foreign currency and are limited.

Developing countries rely on the Western world to buy most of their produce. Any reduction in Western demand would seriously damage their economy.

Basic commodities are exported. Western goods and expertise are imported.

△ The diagram shows how different economies are dependent on international trade.

◁ The photograph shows traders in a futures market in London. Here people can "bet" on the price of a commodity such as soya or sugar, in the future. The futures markets are linked to the price of shares and can make the stock markets even more of a casino.

The relationship of developing countries with the West is complicated. In general the developing countries produce basic commodities such as sugar and rice and the West exports manufactured goods to these countries. The West also provides aid to some countries in the form of loans. But this is not simple charity. Often these loans are made so that goods and machinery can be bought from the lending country. If the crash had led to a recession in the West, then all world economies would have been affected. No economy can be completely isolated from a major stockmarket crash.

Market economics

For 30 years after World War II governments in the West generally believed that they should play a major role in shaping economic policy and ensuring prosperity. Many saw this as the main lesson of the Great Depression of the 1930s, when governments had done little or nothing to stop the mass unemployment that gripped the world.

Economists like John Maynard Keynes believed that such problems could be solved by governments investing money in building roads, improving sewage systems and generally encouraging economic enterprises. These policies prevented the total collapse of the world economy after the war. However, the penalty was increasing price inflation.

By the mid-1970s people began to question the belief that government knows best. Western economies suffered from high inflation and industrial problems. Professor Milton Friedman, also an economist, began to debunk Keynes and argued for "market economics." He said that the way to a healthy economy was by reducing government spending, lowering taxes, and making profit the only factor which would decide whether a company survived or not.

"Opposition"

Opponents of market economics believe that it is a government's responsibility to make sure services and jobs are provided even if this means subsidizing unprofitable industries. For example, they argue an unprofitable railway line should be subsidized if this is the only means of transportation for a community.

▷ The photograph shows a United States' aircraft factory where planes for both civil and military use are being manufactured. These planes are sold producing money for the manufacturers, employment and export orders for the United States. Competitive industries like the aircraft industry produce the nation's wealth.

In the 1970s Milton Freidman, an American economist (far left), argued for a return to "free trade." Margaret Thatcher (left), prime minister of Britain since 1979, is a keen advocate of free trade or market economics.

△ The photograph shows a welfare office in the U.S. where people without work collect welfare benefits. They may have become unemployed as their factories closed down because the products they made could not sell to make large enough profits.

The communist system

In a communist system farms, factories and shops are controlled by the state. Communists have said the problem with the free enterprise system (capitalism) is that there is no control over industry and this leads to a surplus one year, and a shortage the next. Their answer was state planning which could determine how much food should be grown, or how many parts a factory should make. On paper this sounded fine, in practice it has just not worked.

The factory may produce 1,000 parts as planned, but what if only 500 parts can be sold? In a capitalist system a factory that cannot sell its products faces closure. In a communist system the parts continue to be made even if there is a surplus. Elsewhere in the country, products which are really needed do not get produced and there is a shortage.

Inflation in communist countries

In theory there is no inflation in communist countries, just as there is no unemployment. Planning should ensure that just the amount of goods required is produced. In practice there are massive shortages and the state subsidizes all the essential goods like bread and meat. But when this becomes too expensive the price has to be raised. In countries like Poland attempts to raise the price of food have led to riots and the fall of governments.

△ Michail Gorbachev, President of the Soviet Union, is introducing democratic reform and making fundamental economic changes to the system.

△ Markets are common in the Soviet Union and other communist countries. Here some free enterprise is allowed and people use such markets to buy fruit and vegetables.

In recent years communist states have begun to introduce opportunities for private enterprise and are moving towards a more mixed economy. This means that in many areas capitalist-style business functions alongside state-owned industry.

These changes will have a big impact on international trade. In the past there has been a lot of barter trade where, for instance, the Soviet Union imported food in exchange for oil. This is because the currencies of communist countries have been tightly controlled. In the future individual companies will be more likely to determine what they want to import or export.

▽ In Poland, people want the right to belong to a trade union so that they can negotiate with the state about how much money they earn for the work done. The photograph shows Lech Walesa addressing a meeting in support of the banned trade union, Solidarity.

Developing countries

▽ Developing countries in debt may not have the money to tackle famine and drought.

In the 1970s, the poorer, generally non-white countries of the world made a major push to develop their industries. As they tried to do this, ideas began to change about how such developments should take place. Since World War II it was believed that this could best be carried out by government money and central state planning. This was the route taken by India in the 1950s which combined a thriving democracy with socialist planning, funded by aid and international development grants.

But during the late 1960s and 1970s Western banks became flushed with money deposited by oil-producing countries which had benefited from huge rises in the price of oil. The banks had to lend this money to someone and eager borrowers were found in South America and Africa. Now there was greater stress on private enterprise and commercial banks made loans to countries who used the money to build factories and roads.

"Few scourges in human history can claim so many victims as today's debt crisis."
Robert Mugabe
Prime Minister of Zimbabwe
at UNCTAD VII, July 1987

△ Cash crops like cocoa
are grown throughout Africa.
These are often sold to the
Western world – even in areas
where there is famine.

▽ The developing countries
have developed heavy
industries like this aluminum
smelting plant in Ghana. They
often borrow money to do so.

The crash itself had no effect on developing
countries since most are not part of the
international stock market community. But
should the markets continue to be jittery and if
this affects confidence in the Western world,
then there will be less demand for goods from
developing countries and this would have an
immediate impact. Consequently, developing
countries cannot be insulated from major world
economic change.

Debt

The enthusiasm for
lending to developing
countries was not
matched by the skill
needed to manage the
borrowed money. By the
early 1980s many
countries involved just
did not have the money
to pay the interest on
the loans – nor could
they pay back the loans.
Today many
governments argue that
help should be given as
grants rather than loans.

Could it happen again?

So can another crash happen? Of course, booms and busts are part of the stock markets. However the crash of 1987 was different because of the speed with which it happened. It was also different because of the cracks it revealed in the world system. These showed that the 24 hour stock exchange could be dangerously unstable.

At one end there was the Hong Kong exchange which had no regulations at all and was almost like a gambler's den. At the other end there was Tokyo which was tightly controlled by the Japanese government. In between there were many national exchanges trying to play at being international without any proper, universally accepted international standards.

▽ Back to the 1930s? A dealer in London despairs at the news of share collapse on Black Monday. But unlike 1929, the markets show signs of a quick recovery.

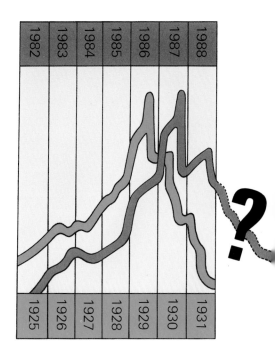

In the United States official reports suggested solutions to control the financial markets. Many of these have been ignored. But many countries have produced encouraging economic results which show that the crash has not led to a worldwide recession.

But on the wider question of the U.S. budget and trade deficits, nothing has been done. The election of George Bush as U.S. president leaves matters unclear. Bush is determined not to raise taxes, which is considered by many to be essential if the U.S. deficits are to be trimmed. So the world's money system remains unstable. Any strong gust of wind could topple it and produce an even bigger crash.

△ The graph shows how the pattern of today's shares is parallel to the movement which caused the Crash of 1929.

Money facts

Growth

The growth of a country is measured in terms of Gross National Product (GNP). This consists of:-

(1) the total value of goods and services produced by a country in any one period — generally either a year or a quarter.

(2) the income that residents of the country may have received as a result of overseas investments minus any income earned by foreigners from that country.

Every quarter GNP figures are issued which compare that quarter's or that year's growth with the previous period. This comparison is expressed as a percentage. Growth is important because it means the economy is expanding, there are more jobs, more money and greater prosperity all round. Politicians campaign on policies which will provide more growth though some people maintain that uncontrolled growth can lead to inflation, particularly if a government relaxes its credit policy and allows people to borrow money easily. Achieving growth without inflation can often prove difficult. Germany has consistently had high growth, and so has Britain recently. The United States economy continues to grow, despite the trade gap.

The government's wealth and taxes

Governments get money by taxing people's money. The taxes can take various forms. Some are direct taxes like income tax. Others are indirect, like VAT or sales taxes on most purchases. Such taxes are generally collected by the central government of a country. However in the United States and countries which have a federal structure, there can be local sales taxes.

In addition, there are special taxes on certain goods and activities, like duties on cars and taxes on cigarettes and drinks. Local governments also raise local taxes. All these taxes go to government and help it to finance its various activities like road building, running schools, defense, payments of pensions and collecting taxes.

Most governments also own companies which make profits. Critics of government ownership of industry say that government should not be running any industry, especially not businesses that are in trouble. They say that taxes are too high and that business can only prosper if taxes are cut.

Others maintain that governments have a role to play in the economy and that taxes can help redistribute wealth, that is, take money from the rich and give to the poor to ensure their welfare.

Dow-Jones Index

The correct term is the Dow-Jones Averages and that is what they are — averages of stock prices in the United States.

It is easy to see when an individual stock price has gone up or down, but how can one know what is going on in the whole stock market? The Dow-Jones Averages are supposed to provide a guide.

There are actually four Dow-Jones averages — one for industrial stocks, one for transportation stocks, one for utilities, and a composite one that is supposed to reflect the status of the other three.

The most famous one, and one that is always quoted, is the Dow-Jones Industrial Average. This is based on 30 leading industrial stocks. But it does not accurately reflect the many hundreds of smaller companies on the market. Despite this the Dow-Jones remains the bible.

Similarly in the United Kingdom there is the *Financial Times* 30-Share Index, though it has been superseded in importance and accuracy by the *Financial Times* 100-Share Index. This is now quoted more often as a shorthand to indicate whether stock prices have gone up or down.

Since these guides are an average, even if the Dow-Jones has gone up, individual stock prices could go down.

Glossary

Stock A stock is a piece of paper which makes the individual who owns it (investor) part owner of a company. It entitles the investor to a share of the company's profits, usually provided through annual dividend payments. Investors can sell stocks at any time but, depending on how the company is doing, they may get more or less than what they paid for the stock. If the company makes losses and closes down, then the stock-holder cannot recover the money paid for the stock. The company uses the money raised by selling stocks to finance new projects or to invest in new machinery.

Inflation Inflation means a regular increase in prices without an increase in production. A skirt worth $50 today may be worth $55 next year, an increase of 10 percent. In the 1970s, when the oil producers suddenly increased their prices, inflation was at its worst. This increase took everyone by surprise. Many industries use oil and the price rise was quickly passed on to the consumer as higher prices.

Currency Currency is the notes and coins used by a particular country as its medium of exchange. When you travel overseas you have to exchange currency. The "rate of exchange" (how many dollars to the pound or yen) depends on the state of the two countries' economies relative to each other.

Interest rate This is the rate which determines how much you have to pay if you want to borrow money. There is a general rate which all the major banks follow called the "base rate." This determines other interest rates, like mortgage interest rates. If the base rate goes up, so do all other interest rates.

Capitalism Under this system, individuals can own stores, factories, other business enterprises and property. The system is regulated by the changing needs of the consumer. However, critics say that those too poor to be consumers are left behind by the system. In practice most capitalist systems do include state owned industries or services as part of a "mixed" economy.

Communism This is the exact opposite of capitalism where everything is owned by the state which then determines wages and prices. In practice this has led to shortages and a lower standard of living than in the West. Today, communism is being modified to accommodate incentive and enterprise that form such an essential part of capitalism.

Reserves This is the sum of money and gold a country has in order to finance its international trade. It is like a country's bank balance. Reserves are also used to make sure that the value of a country's currency stays in line. For instance, if you suddenly got fewer yen in exchange for dollars, then the U.S. government would use its reserves to buy dollars and so increase the dollar's value. A country's reserves may consist of its own currency plus other international currencies like pounds, dollars, French francs, German marks, and yen. Despite the problems with the dollar it still remains the most important international currency in any country's reserves.

Index

A   aid 21

B   balance of trade 6, 7
banks 12, 14, 17
Black Monday 4, 8, 11
borrowing 6, 7, 14, 18
budget deficit 6, 18, 29

C   capitalism 20, 22, 24, 31
communist countries 20,
24-25, 31
computers 8
consumer spending 18
Crash of 1929 4, 6, 8, 12,
29
credit 14
credit cards 8, 14, 15
currency 4, 12-13, 15, 25,
31

D   dealing rooms 8
debt 26-27
depression 4, 22
devaluation 6
developing countries 21,
26-27

E   exchange rate controls
14, 20, 25
exchange rates 12

F   free trade 20, 24
Friedman, Milton 22

G   Gorbachev, Michail 24
governments 6, 8, 12, 13,
14, 16, 18, 20, 22, 26

H   housing 17

I   import controls 6, 14
imports 6, 14, 18
India 26
inflation 13, 15, 16, 17,
22, 24, 31
inflation rate 16
interest rates 4, 12, 13,
27, 31
investors 4, 6
investment 18, 22
investment effect 10, 11
invisible earnings 6

J   Japan 8, 18, 28
jobs 10

K   Keynes, John Maynard 22

L   loans and grants 21, 26

M   market economics 20, 22
military spending 18
money crisis 4, 6, 7
money markets 12
money supply 12, 13, 14,
16
money system 10, 11, 12,
20-21, 29

P   Poland 24, 25
profits 4, 18, 22, 23
program trading 8
public services 10
public spending 14, 18,
22

R   Reagan, Ronald 18
recession 6, 11, 21, 29
regulation 8
reserves 6, 13, 31

S   savings 14, 17
Soviet Union 20, 24, 25
speculation 12, 13
state planning 24-25, 26
stock markets 8, 11, 13,
20, 21, 27, 28
stock prices 4, 8, 10, 11,
29
stocks 4, 31
subsidies 7, 22

T   taxes 10, 14, 18, 22, 29
technology 8
trade 4, 6, 7, 12, 18-19,
20, 25
trade deficit 6, 18, 29
trade gap 19
trade surplus 6
trade unions 25
trading system 12

U   unemployment 6, 7, 22,
23, 24
United States 6, 11, 14,
18-19, 29

W   Walesa, Lech 25
Wall Street 4, 6, 11, 12
wealth 10, 22
wealth effect 10,11

Photographic credits:
Cover and pages 4-5, 28 and back cover:
Topham Picture Library; page 6: Zefa; pages 7,
8-9, 13, 14-15, 17, 19 (both), 20, 22 (right), 23
(both), and 27 (top): Rex Features; pages
10-11, 16, 18 (top) and 26-27: Hutchison
Library; pages 12 and 22 (left): Keystone;
pages 18 (bottom), 24 (left), 25 and 29: Frank
Spooner Agency; pages 24 (right) and 26:
Format Photographers.